Croctober: Asian Style - Volume One

by Jenny Koo

Title: Croctober: Asian Style - Volume One

Introduction:
- Briefly introduce the concept of the "Croctober: Asian Style" series.
- Mention the appeal of Asian flavors and convenience of crockpot cooking.
- Encourage readers to explore the delicious recipes in this volume.

Chapter 1: Appetizers and Starters
- Spicy Edamame
- Miso Soup with Tofu and Seaweed
- Thai Coconut Soup
- Soy-Ginger Meatballs

Chapter 2: Chicken Dishes
- Teriyaki Chicken
- General Tso's Chicken
- Lemongrass Chicken
- Korean BBQ Chicken

Chapter 3: Beef and Pork Delights
- Szechuan Beef
- Pork Adobo
- Beef and Broccoli
- Vietnamese Caramel Pork

Chapter 4: Seafood Specials
- Coconut-Lime Tilapia
- Korean Spicy Salmon
- Sweet and Sour Pineapple Tofu (Vegetarian)
- Thai Red Curry Shrimp

Chapter 5: Vegetable and Tofu Creations

- Mapo Tofu (Vegan)
- Vegetable Thai Green Curry (Vegan)
- Sesame Ginger Tofu (Vegan)
- Vegetable and Chickpea Korma (Vegan)

Chapter 6: Noodle and Rice Dishes

- Pad Thai
- Beef Pho
- Teriyaki Beef Stir-Fry Noodles
- Chinese Five-Spice Pulled Pork
- Indian Coconut Rice Pudding (Dessert)

Conclusion:

- Summarize the variety of Asian crockpot recipes included in this volume.
- Encourage readers to try out different recipes and enjoy a month of delicious Asian-style dishes in October.

Bonus: We Include Blank Recipe Cards Templates and Notes Sections for Your Own Cooking Journals. Be Creative. Explore the Endless Possibilities and Create Your Own. Feel Free to Reproduce the Templates for your Own Use.

- Briefly introduce the concept of the "Croctober: Asian Style" series.

Hey there, foodies and flavor adventurers! 🍜
Welcome to "Croctober: Asian Style," a journey through the tantalizing world of Asian cuisine right from the comfort of your crockpot. 🔪

Picture this: cool October evenings, cozy sweaters, and the irresistible aroma of your favorite Asian dishes wafting through your kitchen. That's the magic of "Croctober." 🍂

We've cooked up something special for you—25 mouthwatering Asian-inspired recipes that will make your taste buds dance with joy. Whether you're a novice in the kitchen or a seasoned chef, there's something here for everyone. 🎉

Why Asian cuisine, you ask? Well, it's all about the perfect blend of flavors—sweet, spicy, savory, and umami—all coming together harmoniously in one delicious dish. And what's better than letting your crockpot do all the hard work while you sit back, relax, and savor every bite? 🥥

Throughout this series, we'll explore the rich tapestry of Asian flavors, from the vibrant street food of Thailand to the soul-warming stews of Korea, and everything in between. It's a culinary adventure that will transport you to bustling markets, family kitchens, and street-side stalls across Asia. 🌏

So, grab your apron, dust off that crockpot, and get ready to embark on a flavorful journey like no other. "Croctober: Asian Style" is all about simplicity, convenience, and most importantly, the joy of sharing a homemade meal with loved ones. 🥡

Get ready to create delicious memories and savor the essence of Asian cuisine, one crockpot recipe at a time. Your culinary adventure begins now! ⭐

- Mention the appeal of Asian flavors and convenience of crockpot cooking.

Now, let's dive a little deeper into why "Croctober: Asian Style" is a match made in culinary heaven.

The Magic of Asian Flavors

Asian cuisine is a treasure trove of flavors that never fails to amaze. It's a symphony of taste and texture, a blend of sweet, spicy, sour, and savory notes that ignite the senses. Whether you're a fan of the fiery spices of Szechuan, the aromatic herbs of Thai cuisine, or the delicate balance of Japanese dishes, Asian flavors have an undeniable allure.

And the best part? You don't need a passport to experience these culinary wonders. With "Croctober: Asian Style," we bring the essence of Asia right into your kitchen. From the complex and vibrant curries to the comforting soups and tenderly cooked meats, every recipe captures the heart and soul of Asian cuisine.

The Beauty of Crockpot Cooking

Now, let's talk convenience. We get it; life can be hectic, and finding time to prepare a homemade meal can be a challenge. That's where your trusty crockpot comes to the rescue. It's like having your own kitchen assistant, working diligently while you go about your day.

Crockpot cooking is all about simplicity. You toss in your ingredients, set it, and forget it. No need for fancy kitchen gadgets or constant supervision. Just let the magic happen as the flavors meld together, creating dishes that are nothing short of extraordinary. It's not just a cooking method; it's a lifestyle, and it's about to become your new best friend in the kitchen.

Why "Croctober"?

So, why did we choose October for this culinary adventure? Well, there's something enchanting about the crisp fall air and the changing leaves that makes it the perfect time to explore new flavors. Plus, as the days get shorter, the allure of a warm, home-cooked meal becomes all the more irresistible. 🍁

With "Croctober: Asian Style," we're bringing you the best of both worlds—the captivating flavors of Asia and the convenience of crockpot cooking. It's a match that will make your October unforgettable. 🎃

So, are you ready to embark on this culinary journey? The adventure begins as soon as you open this book. Let's get cooking! 🍴

- Encourage readers to explore the delicious recipes in this volume.

The Delicious Adventure Awaits! ⭐

We've teased your taste buds with the promise of flavorful Asian dishes, and now it's time to take the plunge into culinary bliss. 🍜

Why We Love These Recipes 🖤

These recipes aren't just about sustenance; they're about indulgence. They're about taking a moment to savor the little pleasures in life, whether it's the first bite of a perfectly seasoned dish or the comforting aroma that fills your home as it simmers in the crockpot. 🏡

Our collection of 25 Asian-style crockpot recipes is designed to spark joy in your kitchen. They celebrate the joys of cooking, the pleasures of sharing a meal with loved ones, and the thrill of discovering new flavors. Each recipe is a little culinary adventure, and we invite you to join us on this journey. 🌏

For All Skill Levels 🔍

Whether you're a seasoned chef or a kitchen newbie, you'll find these recipes approachable and rewarding. We've simplified the steps and included tips and tricks to ensure your culinary success. Don't be shy; give it a try! 🙌

Share the Love 🖤

Cooking is not just about nourishing the body; it's also about nourishing the soul and creating memorable moments with family and friends. So, don't hesitate to share your culinary creations with those you care about. 🍴

The Power of Variety 🍚

Our "Croctober: Asian Style" series is as diverse as the continent it celebrates. From aromatic Thai curries to savory Chinese stir-fries and everything in between, you'll discover a world of flavors in this volume. So why limit yourself to just one recipe when you can explore them all? 

Let's Get Started! 🚀

The adventure begins with the turn of the page. It's time to explore, experiment, and enjoy. We encourage you to make these recipes your own, adapt them to your taste, and most importantly, have fun in the kitchen. 🩶

So, grab your apron, gather your ingredients, and embark on a culinary journey like no other. Your kitchen is your canvas, and these recipes are your palette. Get ready to create delicious memories, one crockpot dish at a time. 🎨

Chapter 1: Appetizers and Starters

- Spicy Edamame
- Miso Soup with Tofu and Seaweed
- Thai Coconut Soup
- Soy-Ginger Meatballs

Title: Spicy Edamame

List of Ingredients:

- 2 cups of frozen edamame (unshelled)
- 2 tablespoons of soy sauce
- 1 tablespoon of sesame oil
- 1 teaspoon of sriracha sauce (adjust to taste)
- 1 clove of garlic, minced
- 1 teaspoon of sesame seeds (for garnish)
- Sliced green onions (for garnish)
- Lime wedges (for garnish)

Nutrition Benefits:

- Edamame is a great source of plant-based protein and fiber.
- Soy sauce adds a savory umami flavor.
- Sesame oil provides healthy fats and nutty richness.
- Sriracha sauce adds a spicy kick.

Calories Count per Serving: Approximately 120 calories per serving

Time Required:

- Preparation: 5 minutes
- Cooking: 2 hours in the crockpot

Total Time Required: 2 hours and 5 minutes

Step-by-Step Instructions:

1. In a bowl, combine the soy sauce, sesame oil, sriracha sauce, and minced garlic. This will be your flavorful marinade.
2. Place the frozen edamame in your crockpot.
3. Pour the marinade over the edamame and stir to coat them evenly. Make sure they're well coated in the delicious flavors.
4. Cover the crockpot and set it to cook on low for 2 hours. The slow cooking will allow the edamame to absorb the flavors and become tender.
5. Once the edamame are cooked, remove them from the crockpot and transfer them to a serving dish.
6. Garnish with sesame seeds, sliced green onions, and lime wedges for an extra burst of flavor and presentation.
7. Serve your Spicy Edamame hot as a fantastic appetizer or snack that's sure to impress your guests!

Title: Miso Soup with Tofu and Seaweed

List of Ingredients:

- 4 cups of vegetable broth
- 3 tablespoons of white miso paste
- 1 cup of sliced tofu
- 2 sheets of nori seaweed, torn into pieces
- 2 green onions, thinly sliced
- 1 tablespoon of soy sauce
- 1 teaspoon of sesame oil
- Pinch of red pepper flakes (optional)
- Fresh cilantro leaves (for garnish)

Nutrition Benefits:

- Miso paste adds probiotics and savory flavor.
- Tofu provides plant-based protein.
- Seaweed is rich in minerals and umami taste.
- Green onions offer a mild onion flavor.

Calories Count per Serving: Approximately 90 calories per serving

Time Required:

- Preparation: 10 minutes
- Cooking: 2 hours in the crockpot

Total Time Required: 2 hours and 10 minutes

Step-by-Step Instructions:

1. In a bowl, whisk together the vegetable broth and white miso paste until well combined. This is your miso broth.
2. Add the miso broth, sliced tofu, torn nori seaweed, and thinly sliced green onions to your crockpot.
3. Stir in the soy sauce, sesame oil, and a pinch of red pepper flakes if you want a bit of heat.
4. Cover the crockpot and cook on low for 2 hours. This slow cooking infuses the flavors beautifully.
5. Ladle the Miso Soup into bowls, garnish with fresh cilantro leaves, and serve hot. Enjoy the comforting warmth and umami goodness!

Title: Thai Coconut Soup

List of Ingredients:

- 1 can (14 oz) of coconut milk
- 4 cups of chicken or vegetable broth
- 2 chicken breasts (or tofu for a vegetarian option), sliced
- 1 red bell pepper, sliced
- 1 carrot, sliced
- 1 onion, chopped
- 2 tablespoons of Thai red curry paste
- 1 tablespoon of fish sauce (or soy sauce for a vegetarian option)
- 1 tablespoon of brown sugar
- Juice of 1 lime
- Fresh cilantro leaves and lime wedges (for garnish)

Nutrition Benefits:

- Coconut milk adds creaminess and healthy fats.
- Bell pepper and carrot provide vitamins and color.
- Thai curry paste offers bold and spicy flavor.
- Lime juice adds a zesty kick.

Calories Count per Serving: Approximately 350 calories per serving

Time Required:

- Preparation: 15 minutes
- Cooking: 4 hours in the crockpot

Total Time Required: 4 hours and 15 minutes

Step-by-Step Instructions:

1. In a large bowl, mix the coconut milk, chicken or vegetable broth, Thai red curry paste, fish sauce (or soy sauce), and brown sugar. This is your flavorful soup base.
2. Place the sliced chicken (or tofu) in your crockpot.
3. Add the sliced red bell pepper, carrot, and chopped onion on top of the chicken (or tofu).
4. Pour the soup base over the ingredients in the crockpot and stir to combine.
5. Cover the crockpot and cook on low for 4 hours.
6. Just before serving, add the juice of one lime to brighten up the flavors.
7. Ladle the Thai Coconut Soup into bowls, garnish with fresh cilantro leaves and lime wedges, and savor the rich, aromatic taste of Thailand in a bowl!

Title: Soy-Ginger Meatballs

List of Ingredients:

- 1 lb ground beef or ground pork (or plant-based meat substitute)
- 1/2 cup breadcrumbs (or gluten-free breadcrumbs)
- 1/4 cup soy sauce
- 2 tablespoons grated ginger
- 2 cloves of garlic, minced
- 2 green onions, finely chopped
- 2 tablespoons sesame seeds
- 1 egg (or flaxseed egg for a vegan option)
- 1/4 cup water
- Cooking spray or oil (for greasing the crockpot)

Nutrition Benefits:

- Ground meat provides protein.
- Ginger adds a spicy and aromatic note.
- Soy sauce contributes a savory flavor.
- Green onions offer a mild onion taste.

Calories Count per Serving: Approximately 150 calories per serving

Time Required:

- Preparation: 15 minutes
- Cooking: 2 hours in the crockpot

Total Time Required: 2 hours and 15 minutes

Step-by-Step Instructions:

1. In a mixing bowl, combine the ground meat (or plant-based meat substitute), breadcrumbs, soy sauce, grated ginger, minced garlic, finely chopped green onions, sesame seeds, and the egg (or flaxseed egg for a vegan option). Mix until all ingredients are well incorporated.
2. Shape the mixture into meatballs, about 1 to 1.5 inches in diameter.
3. Grease the bottom of your crockpot with cooking spray or oil to prevent sticking.
4. Place the meatballs in the crockpot and pour 1/4 cup of water over them.
5. Cover the crockpot and cook on low for 2 hours, allowing the meatballs to become tender and flavorful.
6. Serve your Soy-Ginger Meatballs as a delightful appetizer or pair them with rice or noodles for a satisfying meal. Enjoy the savory goodness!

Chapter 2: Chicken Dishes

- Teriyaki Chicken
- General Tso's Chicken
- Lemongrass Chicken
- Korean BBQ Chicken

Title: Teriyaki Chicken

List of Ingredients:
- 4 boneless, skinless chicken breasts
- 1/2 cup of soy sauce
- 1/4 cup of brown sugar
- 1/4 cup of mirin (rice wine)
- 2 cloves of garlic, minced
- 1 tablespoon of grated fresh ginger
- 1/4 teaspoon of red pepper flakes (adjust to taste)
- 2 tablespoons of cornstarch
- 2 tablespoons of water
- Sliced green onions and sesame seeds (for garnish)
- Steamed white rice (for serving)

Nutrition Benefits:
- Chicken breast is a lean source of protein.
- Soy sauce provides a salty umami flavor.
- Ginger and garlic add aromatic and spicy notes.
- Mirin and brown sugar create a sweet and savory teriyaki sauce.

Calories Count per Serving: Approximately 280 calories per serving (excluding rice)

Time Required:
- Preparation: 15 minutes
- Cooking: 4 hours in the crockpot

Total Time Required: 4 hours and 15 minutes

Step-by-Step Instructions:

1. In a mixing bowl, combine the soy sauce, brown sugar, mirin, minced garlic, grated ginger, and red pepper flakes. This is your teriyaki sauce.
2. Place the boneless, skinless chicken breasts in your crockpot.
3. Pour the teriyaki sauce over the chicken breasts, ensuring they are well coated.
4. Cover the crockpot and cook on low for 4 hours, allowing the chicken to absorb the flavors and become tender.
5. About 30 minutes before serving, mix cornstarch and water in a small bowl to create a slurry. Stir the slurry into the crockpot to thicken the sauce.
6. Serve the Teriyaki Chicken over steamed white rice, garnished with sliced green onions and sesame seeds. It's a delightful balance of sweet and savory!

Title: General Tso's Chicken

List of Ingredients:
- 2 lbs boneless, skinless chicken thighs, cut into bite-sized pieces
- 1/2 cup of hoisin sauce
- 1/4 cup of soy sauce
- 1/4 cup of rice vinegar
- 1/4 cup of brown sugar
- 2 cloves of garlic, minced
- 1 tablespoon of grated fresh ginger
- 1/4 teaspoon of red pepper flakes (adjust to taste)
- 2 tablespoons of cornstarch
- 2 tablespoons of water
- Sliced green onions and sesame seeds (for garnish)
- Cooked white or brown rice (for serving)

Nutrition Benefits:
- Chicken thighs offer a juicier and flavorful cut of meat.
- Hoisin sauce provides a sweet and savory base.
- Rice vinegar adds a tangy note.
- Garlic, ginger, and red pepper flakes create depth and heat.

Calories Count per Serving: Approximately 350 calories per serving (excluding rice)

Time Required:
- Preparation: 20 minutes
- Cooking: 3 hours in the crockpot

Total Time Required: 3 hours and 20 minutes

Step-by-Step Instructions:

1. In a mixing bowl, whisk together hoisin sauce, soy sauce, rice vinegar, brown sugar, minced garlic, grated ginger, and red pepper flakes to create your General Tso's sauce.

2. Place the bite-sized chicken pieces in your crockpot.

3. Pour the General Tso's sauce over the chicken and stir to ensure even coating.

4. Cover the crockpot and cook on low for 3 hours, allowing the chicken to become tender and absorb the flavors.

5. About 30 minutes before serving, mix cornstarch and water in a small bowl to create a slurry. Stir the slurry into the crockpot to thicken the sauce.

6. Serve General Tso's Chicken over cooked rice, garnished with sliced green onions and sesame seeds. It's a delicious takeout favorite made right at home!

Title: Lemongrass Chicken

List of Ingredients:
- 4 boneless, skinless chicken thighs
- 2 stalks of lemongrass, chopped into pieces
- 1 onion, chopped
- 3 cloves of garlic, minced
- 1 thumb-sized piece of fresh ginger, sliced
- 1/4 cup of chicken broth
- 2 tablespoons of fish sauce (or soy sauce for a vegetarian option)
- 2 tablespoons of brown sugar
- 1 teaspoon of chili paste (adjust to taste)
- Fresh cilantro leaves and lime wedges (for garnish)
- Cooked jasmine rice (for serving)

Nutrition Benefits:
- Chicken thighs provide a richer flavor and tenderness.
- Lemongrass adds a citrusy and aromatic note.
- Ginger and garlic enhance the flavor profile.
- Fish sauce contributes depth and umami.
-

Calories Count per Serving: Approximately 280 calories per serving (excluding rice)

Time Required:
- Preparation: 15 minutes
- Cooking: 3 hours in the crockpot

Total Time Required: 3 hours and 15 minutes

Step-by-Step Instructions:

1. Place the boneless, skinless chicken thighs in your crockpot.

2. In a blender or food processor, combine chopped lemongrass, chopped onion, minced garlic, sliced ginger, chicken broth, fish sauce (or soy sauce), brown sugar, and chili paste. Blend until you have a smooth lemongrass marinade.

3. Pour the lemongrass marinade over the chicken thighs, ensuring they are well coated.

4. Cover the crockpot and cook on low for 3 hours, allowing the flavors to infuse into the chicken.

5. Once cooked, remove the chicken from the crockpot and slice it into strips.

6. Serve Lemongrass Chicken over cooked jasmine rice, garnished with fresh cilantro leaves and lime wedges. It's a zesty and aromatic delight!

Title: Korean BBQ Chicken

List of Ingredients:

- 4 boneless, skinless chicken thighs
- 1/2 cup of Korean BBQ sauce
- 2 tablespoons of soy sauce
- 2 cloves of garlic, minced
- 1 tablespoon of grated fresh ginger
- 2 tablespoons of brown sugar
- Sliced green onions and sesame seeds (for garnish)
- Cooked short-grain or jasmine rice (for serving)
-

Nutrition Benefits:

- Chicken thighs provide succulent and tender meat.
- Korean BBQ sauce offers a sweet and savory profile.
- Garlic and ginger add aromatic and spicy notes.
-

Calories Count per Serving: Approximately 250 calories per serving (excluding rice)

Time Required:

- Preparation: 10 minutes
- Cooking: 3 hours in the crockpot

Total Time Required: 3 hours and 10 minutes

Step-by-Step Instructions:

1. Place the boneless, skinless chicken thighs in your crockpot.

2. In a bowl, whisk together the Korean BBQ sauce, soy sauce, minced garlic, grated ginger, and brown sugar. This is your flavorful Korean BBQ marinade.

3. Pour the Korean BBQ marinade over the chicken thighs, ensuring they are well coated.

4. Cover the crockpot and cook on low for 3 hours, allowing the chicken to soak up the delicious Korean flavors.

5. Once cooked, remove the chicken from the crockpot and slice it into bite-sized pieces.

6. Serve Korean BBQ Chicken over cooked short-grain or jasmine rice, garnished with sliced green onions and sesame seeds. It's a taste of Korea that's sweet, savory, and simply irresistible!

Chapter 3: Beef and Pork Delights

- Szechuan Beef

- Pork Adobo

- Beef and Broccoli

- Vietnamese Caramel Pork

Title: Szechuan Beef

List of Ingredients:
- 2 lbs beef sirloin or flank steak, thinly sliced
- 1/4 cup of soy sauce
- 2 tablespoons of hoisin sauce
- 2 tablespoons of Szechuan sauce (adjust to taste)
- 1 tablespoon of honey
- 2 cloves of garlic, minced
- 1 thumb-sized piece of fresh ginger, grated
- 1/2 cup of beef broth
- 2 bell peppers (red and green), sliced
- 1 cup of broccoli florets
- 1 tablespoon of cornstarch
- 2 tablespoons of water
- Sliced green onions and sesame seeds (for garnish)
- Cooked white rice (for serving)

Nutrition Benefits:
- Beef provides a rich source of protein and iron.
- Bell peppers and broccoli offer vitamins and color.
- Soy sauce and Szechuan sauce create a savory and spicy profile.
- Honey adds sweetness and balance.

Calories Count per Serving: Approximately 350 calories per serving (excluding rice)

Time Required:
- Preparation: 20 minutes
- Cooking: 4 hours in the crockpot

Total Time Required: 4 hours and 20 minutes

Step-by-Step Instructions:

1. In a bowl, combine the soy sauce, hoisin sauce, Szechuan sauce, honey, minced garlic, and grated ginger to create your flavorful Szechuan marinade.

2. Place the thinly sliced beef in your crockpot.

3. Pour the Szechuan marinade over the beef slices, ensuring they are well coated.

4. Add beef broth, sliced bell peppers, and broccoli florets to the crockpot, distributing them evenly.

5. Cover the crockpot and cook on low for 4 hours, allowing the beef to become tender and absorb the bold flavors.

6. About 30 minutes before serving, mix cornstarch and water in a small bowl to create a slurry. Stir the slurry into the crockpot to thicken the sauce.

7. Serve Szechuan Beef over cooked white rice, garnished with sliced green onions and sesame seeds. It's a fiery and flavorful delight!

Title: Pork Adobo

List of Ingredients:

- 2 lbs boneless pork shoulder, cut into chunks
- 1 onion, chopped
- 4 cloves of garlic, minced
- 1/4 cup of soy sauce
- 1/4 cup of vinegar
- 1 teaspoon of black peppercorns
- 3 bay leaves
- 1/2 cup of water
- Cooked white or brown rice (for serving)

Nutrition Benefits:

- Pork shoulder offers tender and juicy meat.
- Soy sauce and vinegar create a savory and tangy profile.
- Garlic and black peppercorns add depth of flavor.
- Bay leaves provide aromatic notes.

Calories Count per Serving: Approximately 300 calories per serving (excluding rice)

Time Required:

- Preparation: 10 minutes
- Cooking: 4 hours in the crockpot

Total Time Required: 4 hours and 10 minutes

Step-by-Step Instructions:

1. Place the chunks of boneless pork shoulder in your crockpot.
2. In a bowl, mix together the chopped onion, minced garlic, soy sauce, vinegar, black peppercorns, and bay leaves. This is your Adobo marinade.
3. Pour the Adobo marinade over the pork chunks, ensuring they are well coated.
4. Add 1/2 cup of water to the crockpot to create a flavorful broth.
5. Cover the crockpot and cook on low for 4 hours, allowing the pork to become tender and infused with the rich Adobo flavors.
6. Once cooked, serve Pork Adobo over cooked white or brown rice, allowing the savory sauce to soak into the rice. It's a taste of the Philippines that's hearty and satisfying!

Title: Beef and Broccoli

List of Ingredients:

- 1.5 lbs beef flank steak, thinly sliced
- 1 cup of beef broth
- 1/2 cup of soy sauce
- 1/4 cup of brown sugar
- 3 cloves of garlic, minced
- 2 tablespoons of cornstarch
- 2 tablespoons of water
- 4 cups of broccoli florets
- Cooked white rice (for serving)

Nutrition Benefits:

- Beef flank steak provides lean protein.
- Soy sauce and brown sugar create a sweet and savory teriyaki-style sauce.
- Garlic adds aromatic depth of flavor.
- Broccoli offers vitamins and a vibrant green color.

Calories Count per Serving: Approximately 320 calories per serving (excluding rice)

Time Required:

- Preparation: 15 minutes
- Cooking: 4 hours in the crockpot

Total Time Required: 4 hours and 15 minutes

Step-by-Step Instructions:

1. Place the thinly sliced beef flank steak in your crockpot.
2. In a bowl, whisk together beef broth, soy sauce, brown sugar, and minced garlic to create a flavorful sauce.
3. Pour the sauce over the beef slices, ensuring they are well coated.
4. Add the broccoli florets to the crockpot, distributing them evenly.
5. Cover the crockpot and cook on low for 4 hours, allowing the beef to become tender and the broccoli to absorb the delicious sauce.
6. About 30 minutes before serving, mix cornstarch and water in a small bowl to create a slurry. Stir the slurry into the crockpot to thicken the sauce.
7. Serve Beef and Broccoli over cooked white rice. It's a classic favorite that's simple, delicious, and nutritious!

Title: Vietnamese Caramel Pork

List of Ingredients:

- 2 lbs pork shoulder, cut into chunks
- 1 cup of water
- 1/4 cup of fish sauce
- 1/4 cup of brown sugar
- 3 cloves of garlic, minced
- 1 thumb-sized piece of fresh ginger, sliced
- 2 star anise pods
- Sliced green onions (for garnish)
- Cooked jasmine rice (for serving)

Nutrition Benefits:

- Pork shoulder offers tender and flavorful meat.
- Fish sauce and brown sugar create a sweet and savory caramel sauce.
- Garlic and ginger add aromatic depth.
- Star anise provides a hint of licorice-like flavor.

Calories Count per Serving: Approximately 300 calories per serving (excluding rice)

Time Required:

- Preparation: 10 minutes
- Cooking: 4 hours in the crockpot

Total Time Required: 4 hours and 10 minutes

Step-by-Step Instructions:

1. Place the chunks of pork shoulder in your crockpot.
2. In a bowl, whisk together water, fish sauce, brown sugar, minced garlic, sliced ginger, and star anise to create your flavorful caramel sauce.
3. Pour the caramel sauce over the pork chunks, ensuring they are well coated.
4. Cover the crockpot and cook on low for 4 hours, allowing the pork to become tender and absorb the sweet and savory caramel flavors.
5. Once cooked, remove the pork from the crockpot and discard the star anise.
6. Serve Vietnamese Caramel Pork over cooked jasmine rice, garnished with sliced green onions. It's a taste of Vietnam that's both exotic and comforting!

Chapter 4: Seafood Specials

- Coconut-Lime Tilapia
- Korean Spicy Salmon
- Sweet and Sour Pineapple Tofu (Vegetarian)
- Thai Red Curry Shrimp

Title: Coconut-Lime Tilapia

List of Ingredients:

- 4 tilapia fillets
- 1 can (14 oz) of coconut milk
- Zest and juice of 1 lime
- 2 cloves of garlic, minced
- 1 thumb-sized piece of fresh ginger, grated
- 1 tablespoon of red curry paste (adjust to taste)
- 1 red bell pepper, sliced
- 1 cup of sliced zucchini
- Fresh cilantro leaves and lime wedges (for garnish)
- Cooked jasmine rice (for serving)

Nutrition Benefits:

- Tilapia offers a mild and flaky fish.
- Coconut milk provides creaminess and healthy fats.
- Lime adds zesty and citrusy notes.
- Red curry paste offers a spicy kick.

Calories Count per Serving: Approximately 280 calories per serving (excluding rice)

Time Required:

- Preparation: 15 minutes
- Cooking: 2.5 hours in the crockpot

Total Time Required: 2 hours and 45 minutes

Step-by-Step Instructions:

1. Place the tilapia filets in your crockpot.
2. In a mixing bowl, whisk together coconut milk, lime zest, lime juice, minced garlic, grated ginger, and red curry paste to create your flavorful coconut-lime sauce.
3. Pour the coconut-lime sauce over the tilapia filets, ensuring they are well coated.
4. Add sliced red bell pepper and sliced zucchini to the crockpot, distributing them evenly.
5. Cover the crockpot and cook on low for 2.5 hours, allowing the tilapia to become tender and absorb the vibrant flavors.
6. Once cooked, serve Coconut-Lime Tilapia over cooked jasmine rice, garnished with fresh cilantro leaves and lime wedges. It's a tropical delight that's both light and satisfying!

Title: Korean Spicy Salmon

List of Ingredients:

- 4 salmon fillets
- 1/4 cup of gochujang (Korean red pepper paste)
- 2 tablespoons of soy sauce
- 2 tablespoons of honey
- 2 cloves of garlic, minced
- 1 thumb-sized piece of fresh ginger, grated
- 2 green onions, thinly sliced
- Sesame seeds (for garnish)
- Cooked brown or white rice (for serving)

Nutrition Benefits:

- Salmon provides heart-healthy omega-3 fatty acids.
- Gochujang adds a spicy and savory Korean flavor.
- Soy sauce and honey create a sweet and umami balance.
- Garlic and ginger add aromatic depth.

Calories Count per Serving: Approximately 350 calories per serving (excluding rice)

Time Required:

- Preparation: 10 minutes
- Cooking: 2 hours in the crockpot

Total Time Required: 2 hours and 10 minutes

Step-by-Step Instructions:

1. Place the salmon filets in your crockpot.
2. In a bowl, mix together gochujang, soy sauce, honey, minced garlic, grated ginger, and half of the thinly sliced green onions to create your spicy Korean marinade.
3. Pour the Korean marinade over the salmon fillets, ensuring they are well coated.
4. Cover the crockpot and cook on low for 2 hours, allowing the salmon to become tender and absorb the spicy and sweet flavors.
5. Once cooked, serve Korean Spicy Salmon over cooked brown or white rice, garnished with the remaining thinly sliced green onions and sesame seeds. It's a fiery and flavorful Korean delight!

Title: Sweet and Sour Pineapple Tofu (Vegetarian)

List of Ingredients:

- 1 block (14 oz) of firm tofu, cubed
- 1 can (14 oz) of pineapple chunks, with juice
- 1/4 cup of rice vinegar
- 1/4 cup of brown sugar
- 2 tablespoons of soy sauce
- 1 red bell pepper, sliced
- 1 green bell pepper, sliced
- 1 onion, chopped
- 1 tablespoon of cornstarch
- 2 tablespoons of water
- Cooked white or brown rice (for serving)

Nutrition Benefits:

- Tofu provides plant-based protein.
- Pineapple adds natural sweetness and vitamin C.
- Rice vinegar and soy sauce create a tangy and savory sauce.
- Bell peppers offer vitamins and color.

Calories Count per Serving: Approximately 280 calories per serving (excluding rice)

Time Required:

- Preparation: 15 minutes
- Cooking: 2.5 hours in the crockpot

Total Time Required: 2 hours and 45 minutes

Step-by-Step Instructions:

1. Place the cubed firm tofu in your crockpot.
2. In a bowl, combine pineapple chunks (with juice), rice vinegar, brown sugar, and soy sauce to create your sweet and sour sauce.
3. Pour the sweet and sour sauce over the tofu, ensuring it's well coated.
4. Add sliced red bell pepper, sliced green bell pepper, and chopped onion to the crockpot, distributing them evenly.
5. Cover the crockpot and cook on low for 2.5 hours, allowing the tofu and vegetables to absorb the delightful sweet and sour flavors.
6. About 30 minutes before serving, mix cornstarch and water in a small bowl to create a slurry. Stir the slurry into the crockpot to thicken the sauce.
7. Serve Sweet and Sour Pineapple Tofu over cooked white or brown rice. It's a vegetarian take on a classic favorite!

Title: Thai Red Curry Shrimp

List of Ingredients:

- 1 lb large shrimp, peeled and deveined
- 1 can (14 oz) of coconut milk
- 2 tablespoons of Thai red curry paste (adjust to taste)
- 1 red bell pepper, sliced
- 1 yellow bell pepper, sliced
- 1 zucchini, sliced
- 1 tablespoon of fish sauce (or soy sauce for a vegetarian option)
- 1 tablespoon of brown sugar
- Fresh cilantro leaves and lime wedges (for garnish)
- Cooked jasmine rice (for serving)

Nutrition Benefits:

- Shrimp provides lean protein.
- Thai red curry paste adds spicy and aromatic notes.
- Coconut milk offers creaminess and healthy fats.
- Bell peppers and zucchini provide vitamins and color.

Calories Count per Serving: Approximately 320 calories per serving (excluding rice)

Time Required:

- Preparation: 15 minutes
- Cooking: 2.5 hours in the crockpot

Total Time Required: 2 hours and 45 minutes

Step-by-Step Instructions:

1. Place the peeled and deveined shrimp in your crockpot.
2. In a bowl, whisk together coconut milk, Thai red curry paste, sliced red bell pepper, sliced yellow bell pepper, sliced zucchini, fish sauce (or soy sauce), and brown sugar to create your flavorful Thai red curry sauce.
3. Pour the Thai red curry sauce over the shrimp, ensuring they are well coated.
4. Cover the crockpot and cook on low for 2.5 hours, allowing the shrimp to become tender and infused with the spicy and creamy Thai flavors.
5. Once cooked, serve Thai Red Curry Shrimp over cooked jasmine rice, garnished with fresh cilantro leaves and lime wedges. It's a taste of Thailand that's both aromatic and exotic!

Chapter 5: Vegetable and Tofu Creations

- Mapo Tofu (Vegan)
- Vegetable Thai Green Curry (Vegan)
- Sesame Ginger Tofu (Vegan)
- Vegetable and Chickpea Korma
  (Vegan)

Title: Mapo Tofu (Vegan)

List of Ingredients:

- 1 block (14 oz) of firm tofu, cubed
- 1 cup of vegetable broth
- 2 tablespoons of soy sauce
- 2 tablespoons of chili bean paste (doubanjiang)
- 2 cloves of garlic, minced
- 1 thumb-sized piece of fresh ginger, grated
- 1 tablespoon of Szechuan peppercorns (adjust to taste)
- 2 green onions, thinly sliced (green parts for garnish)
- Cooked white or brown rice (for serving)

Nutrition Benefits:

- Firm tofu provides plant-based protein.
- Vegetable broth offers a savory base.
- Chili bean paste adds a spicy and umami kick.
- Garlic and ginger add aromatic depth.

Calories Count per Serving: Approximately 220 calories per serving (excluding rice)

Time Required:

- Preparation: 15 minutes
- Cooking: 3 hours in the crockpot

Total Time Required: 3 hours and 15 minutes

Step-by-Step Instructions:

1. Place the cubed firm tofu in your crockpot.

2. In a bowl, whisk together vegetable broth, soy sauce, chili bean paste, minced garlic, grated ginger, and Szechuan peppercorns to create your flavorful Mapo Tofu sauce.

3. Pour the Mapo Tofu sauce over the tofu cubes, ensuring they are well coated.

4. Cover the crockpot and cook on low for 3 hours, allowing the tofu to absorb the bold and spicy flavors.

5. About 30 minutes before serving, stir in most of the thinly sliced green onions, reserving some for garnish.

6. Serve Mapo Tofu over cooked white or brown rice, garnished with the remaining green onions. It's a vegan twist on a classic Szechuan dish that's both fiery and satisfying!

Title: Vegetable Thai Green Curry (Vegan)

List of Ingredients:

- 2 cups of mixed vegetables (e.g., bell peppers, broccoli, carrots)
- 1 can (14 oz) of coconut milk
- 2 tablespoons of Thai green curry paste (adjust to taste)
- 1 tablespoon of soy sauce
- 1 tablespoon of brown sugar
- 1 thumb-sized piece of fresh ginger, sliced
- 1 lime, zest and juice
- Fresh cilantro leaves and lime wedges (for garnish)
- Cooked jasmine rice (for serving)

Nutrition Benefits:

- Mixed vegetables provide vitamins and color.
- Coconut milk offers creaminess and healthy fats.
- Thai green curry paste adds spicy and aromatic notes.
- Ginger and lime add freshness and zing.

Calories Count per Serving: Approximately 250 calories per serving (excluding rice)

Time Required:

- Preparation: 10 minutes
- Cooking: 2.5 hours in the crockpot

Total Time Required: 2 hours and 40 minutes

Step-by-Step Instructions:

1. Place the mixed vegetables in your crockpot.
2. In a bowl, whisk together coconut milk, Thai green curry paste, soy sauce, brown sugar, sliced ginger, lime zest, and lime juice to create your flavorful Thai Green Curry sauce.
3. Pour the Thai Green Curry sauce over the mixed vegetables, ensuring they are well coated.
4. Cover the crockpot and cook on low for 2.5 hours, allowing the vegetables to absorb the creamy and spicy Thai flavors.
5. Once cooked, serve Vegetable Thai Green Curry over cooked jasmine rice, garnished with fresh cilantro leaves and lime wedges. It's a vegan Thai delight that's both comforting and exotic!

Title: Sesame Ginger Tofu (Vegan)

List of Ingredients:

- 1 block (14 oz) of firm tofu, cubed
- 1/4 cup of soy sauce
- 2 tablespoons of rice vinegar
- 2 tablespoons of toasted sesame oil
- 1 thumb-sized piece of fresh ginger, grated
- 2 cloves of garlic, minced
- 2 tablespoons of toasted sesame seeds (for garnish)
- Sliced green onions (for garnish)
- Cooked brown or white rice (for serving)

Nutrition Benefits:

- Firm tofu provides plant-based protein.
- Soy sauce and toasted sesame oil create a savory and nutty sauce.
- Ginger and garlic add aromatic depth.
- Sesame seeds offer crunch and flavor.

Calories Count per Serving: Approximately 260 calories per serving (excluding rice)

Time Required:

- Preparation: 15 minutes
- Cooking: 3 hours in the crockpot

Total Time Required: 3 hours and 15 minutes

Step-by-Step Instructions:

1. Place the cubed firm tofu in your crockpot.
2. In a bowl, whisk together soy sauce, rice vinegar, toasted sesame oil, grated ginger, and minced garlic to create your flavorful Sesame Ginger sauce.
3. Pour the Sesame Ginger sauce over the tofu cubes, ensuring they are well coated.
4. Cover the crockpot and cook on low for 3 hours, allowing the tofu to absorb the savory and nutty flavors.
5. About 30 minutes before serving, sprinkle toasted sesame seeds over the tofu for added crunch and flavor.
6. Serve Sesame Ginger Tofu over cooked brown or white rice, garnished with sliced green onions. It's a vegan dish that's simple, yet bursting with sesame goodness!

Title: Vegetable and Chickpea Korma (Vegan)

List of Ingredients:

- 2 cups of mixed vegetables (e.g., cauliflower, peas, carrots)
- 1 can (14 oz) of chickpeas, drained and rinsed
- 1 can (14 oz) of coconut milk
- 1/4 cup of tomato sauce
- 2 tablespoons of korma curry paste (adjust to taste)
- 2 tablespoons of cashew butter (or almond butter)
- 1 teaspoon of garam masala
- Fresh cilantro leaves (for garnish)
- Cooked basmati rice (for serving)

Nutrition Benefits:

- Mixed vegetables provide vitamins and fiber.
- Chickpeas offer plant-based protein and fiber.
- Coconut milk adds creaminess and healthy fats.
- Korma curry paste and garam masala create a fragrant and spicy profile.

Calories Count per Serving: Approximately 280 calories per serving (excluding rice)

Time Required:

- Preparation: 10 minutes
- Cooking: 2.5 hours in the crockpot

Total Time Required: 2 hours and 40 minutes

Step-by-Step Instructions:

1. Place the mixed vegetables and drained chickpeas in your crockpot.

2. In a bowl, whisk together coconut milk, tomato sauce, korma curry paste, cashew butter (or almond butter), and garam masala to create your flavorful Korma sauce.

3. Pour the Korma sauce over the mixed vegetables and chickpeas, ensuring they are well coated.

4. Cover the crockpot and cook on low for 2.5 hours, allowing the flavors to meld together.

5. Once cooked, serve Vegetable and Chickpea Korma over cooked basmati rice, garnished with fresh cilantro leaves. It's a vegan delight that's rich and aromatic!

Chapter 6: Noodle and Rice Dishes

- Pad Thai
- Beef Pho
- Teriyaki Beef Stir-Fry Noodles
- Chinese Five-Spice Pulled Pork
- Indian Coconut Rice Pudding (Dessert)

Title: Pad Thai

List of Ingredients:

- 8 oz rice noodles
- 2 boneless, skinless chicken breasts, thinly sliced (optional)
- 2 cloves of garlic, minced
- 1 thumb-sized piece of fresh ginger, grated
- 2 eggs, beaten
- 1 cup of bean sprouts
- 1/2 cup of chopped peanuts
- 2 green onions, thinly sliced
- Fresh cilantro leaves (for garnish)
- Lime wedges (for garnish)

Nutrition Benefits:

- Rice noodles provide a gluten-free option.
- Chicken offers lean protein (optional).
- Bean sprouts add crunch and vitamins.
- Peanuts provide healthy fats and protein.

Calories Count per Serving: Approximately 400 calories per serving (excluding garnishes)

Time Required:

- Preparation: 15 minutes
- Cooking: 2 hours in the crockpot

Total Time Required: 2 hours and 15 minutes

Step-by-Step Instructions:

1. Soak the rice noodles in warm water for about 15 minutes or until they become pliable, then drain them.
2. Place the sliced chicken (if using) in your crockpot.
3. Add the soaked and drained rice noodles on top of the chicken.
4. In a bowl, whisk together minced garlic, grated ginger, and beaten eggs.
5. Pour the egg mixture over the noodles, ensuring it's distributed evenly.
6. Cover the crockpot and cook on low for 2 hours, allowing the noodles to cook and the chicken (if using) to become tender.
7. After cooking, gently fluff the noodles with a fork.
8. Serve Pad Thai in bowls, garnished with bean sprouts, chopped peanuts, thinly sliced green onions, fresh cilantro leaves, and lime wedges. It's a classic Thai favorite with a crockpot twist!

Title: Beef Pho

List of Ingredients:
- 1 lb beef flank steak, thinly sliced
- 8 cups of beef broth
- 2 cloves of garlic, minced
- 1 thumb-sized piece of fresh ginger, sliced
- 1 onion, thinly sliced
- 2 cinnamon sticks
- 4 star anise pods
- 4 cloves
- 1 teaspoon of coriander seeds
- Rice noodles (for serving)
- Fresh basil leaves, bean sprouts, lime wedges, and Sriracha (for garnish)

Nutrition Benefits:
- Beef flank steak offers lean protein.
- Beef broth provides a savory base.
- Fresh herbs and lime add freshness and aroma.
- Rice noodles offer a gluten-free option.

Calories Count per Serving: Approximately 350 calories per serving (excluding garnishes)

Time Required:
- Preparation: 15 minutes
- Cooking: 4 hours in the crockpot

Total Time Required: 4 hours and 15 minutes

Step-by-Step Instructions:

1. Place the thinly sliced beef flank steak in your crockpot.
2. In a bowl, combine minced garlic, sliced ginger, thinly sliced onion, cinnamon sticks, star anise pods, cloves, and coriander seeds.
3. Pour the aromatic mixture over the beef.
4. Add the beef broth to the crockpot, ensuring the beef is fully submerged.
5. Cover the crockpot and cook on low for 4 hours, allowing the beef to become tender and the flavors to meld.
6. About 30 minutes before serving, cook rice noodles according to package instructions.
7. Serve Beef Pho in bowls, placing cooked rice noodles at the bottom, followed by the beef and aromatic broth.
8. Garnish with fresh basil leaves, bean sprouts, lime wedges, and Sriracha to taste. It's a comforting Vietnamese classic!

Title: Teriyaki Beef Stir-Fry Noodles

List of Ingredients:

- 1 lb beef sirloin, thinly sliced
- 1 cup of teriyaki sauce
- 2 cloves of garlic, minced
- 1 thumb-sized piece of fresh ginger, grated
- 1 red bell pepper, sliced
- 1 yellow bell pepper, sliced
- 1 zucchini, sliced
- 8 oz udon or soba noodles
- Sliced green onions (for garnish)
- Toasted sesame seeds (for garnish)

Nutrition Benefits:

- Beef sirloin offers lean protein.
- Teriyaki sauce adds a sweet and savory profile.
- Colorful bell peppers and zucchini provide vitamins.
- Udon or soba noodles offer a satisfying base.

Calories Count per Serving: Approximately 400 calories per serving (excluding garnishes)

Time Required:

- Preparation: 15 minutes
- Cooking: 2 hours in the crockpot

Total Time Required: 2 hours and 15 minutes

Step-by-Step Instructions:

1. Place the thinly sliced beef sirloin in your crockpot.
2. In a bowl, mix teriyaki sauce, minced garlic, and grated ginger to create your flavorful Teriyaki marinade.
3. Pour the Teriyaki marinade over the beef slices, ensuring they are well coated.
4. Add sliced red bell pepper, yellow bell pepper, and zucchini to the crockpot, distributing them evenly.
5. Cover the crockpot and cook on low for 2 hours, allowing the beef to absorb the sweet and savory Teriyaki flavors.
6. About 30 minutes before serving, cook udon or soba noodles according to package instructions.
7. Serve Teriyaki Beef Stir-Fry Noodles in bowls, placing cooked noodles at the bottom, followed by the beef and vegetables.
8. Garnish with sliced green onions and toasted sesame seeds for added flavor and texture. It's a delightful Japanese-inspired dish!

Title: Chinese Five-Spice Pulled Pork

List of Ingredients:

- 3 lbs pork shoulder
- 1 onion, chopped
- 1/4 cup of soy sauce
- 2 tablespoons of hoisin sauce
- 2 tablespoons of brown sugar
- 1 teaspoon of Chinese five-spice powder
- 1/2 teaspoon of ground white pepper
- Buns or steamed bao (for serving)
- Pickled vegetables (for garnish)

Nutrition Benefits:

- Pork shoulder offers tender and flavorful meat.
- Chinese five-spice powder adds depth and aroma.
- Hoisin sauce and soy sauce create a sweet and savory profile.
- Pickled vegetables offer a tangy crunch.

Calories Count per Serving: Approximately 350 calories per serving (excluding buns and garnishes)

Time Required:

- Preparation: 15 minutes
- Cooking: 4 hours in the crockpot

Total Time Required: 4 hours and 15 minutes

Step-by-Step Instructions:

1. Place the pork shoulder in your crockpot.
2. In a bowl, combine chopped onion, soy sauce, hoisin sauce, brown sugar, Chinese five-spice powder, and ground white pepper to create your flavorful Chinese Five-Spice marinade.
3. Pour the marinade over the pork shoulder, ensuring it's well coated.
4. Cover the crockpot and cook on low for 4 hours, allowing the pork to become tender and infused with the Chinese five-spice flavors.
5. Once cooked, shred the pulled pork using two forks.
6. Serve Chinese Five-Spice Pulled Pork in buns or steamed bao, garnished with pickled vegetables. It's a fusion of flavors that's both savory and aromatic!

Title: Indian Coconut Rice Pudding (Dessert)

List of Ingredients:

- 1 cup of basmati rice
- 1 can (14 oz) of coconut milk
- 1/2 cup of sugar
- 1/4 teaspoon of cardamom powder
- 1/4 teaspoon of ground cinnamon
- 1/4 cup of raisins
- 1/4 cup of chopped nuts (e.g., almonds, cashews)
- Saffron strands (for garnish, optional)

Nutrition Benefits:

- Basmati rice provides a fragrant and fluffy base.
- Coconut milk adds creaminess and a tropical twist.
- Cardamom and cinnamon offer warm and aromatic notes.
- Raisins and nuts add sweetness and crunch.

Calories Count per Serving: Approximately 250 calories per serving (excluding garnishes)

Time Required:

- Preparation: 10 minutes
- Cooking: 2.5 hours in the crockpot

Total Time Required: 2 hours and 40 minutes

Step-by-Step Instructions:

1. Rinse the basmati rice thoroughly and drain.
2. Place the rinsed rice in your crockpot.
3. In a bowl, mix together coconut milk, sugar, cardamom powder, and ground cinnamon to create your flavorful Coconut Rice Pudding mixture.
4. Pour the Coconut Rice Pudding mixture over the rice, ensuring it's well combined.
5. Add raisins and chopped nuts to the crockpot, distributing them evenly.
6. Cover the crockpot and cook on low for 2.5 hours, allowing the rice to become tender and the flavors to meld.
7. About 30 minutes before serving, if desired, garnish with saffron strands for added color and aroma.
8. Serve Indian Coconut Rice Pudding in bowls. It's a sweet and comforting dessert with an Indian twist!

- Summarize the variety of Asian crockpot recipes included in this volume.

In this volume of "Croctober: Asian Style," we've embarked on a flavorful journey through the heart of Asian cuisine, exploring a diverse array of crockpot recipes that promise to delight your taste buds and simplify your cooking routine. From the comforting classics to inventive twists, our collection features a rich tapestry of flavors and textures.

In the "Noodle and Rice Dishes" chapter, we've divided into beloved Asian favorites like the zesty and aromatic "Pad Thai," the comforting and fragrant "Beef Pho," and the savory-sweet "Teriyaki Beef Stir-Fry Noodles." These dishes showcase the versatility of noodles and rice as they soak up the tantalizing sauces and spices, delivering both comfort and excitement to your dinner table.

If you're craving bold and savory, you'll appreciate the "Chinese Five-Spice Pulled Pork" in our chapter. It offers tender, succulent bites with the mesmerizing flavors of Chinese five-spice, hoisin, and soy sauce, perfect for crafting mouthwatering sandwiches or bao.

And for dessert, we haven't forgotten to sweeten your palate with the "Indian Coconut Rice Pudding." This delightful treat infuses the fragrant aroma of cardamom and cinnamon into creamy coconut rice, creating a dessert that's both soothing and indulgent.

Throughout this volume, we've celebrated the ease and convenience of crockpot cooking while honoring the intricate and diverse tastes of Asian cuisine. Whether you're a fan of Thai, Vietnamese, Japanese, Chinese, or Indian flavors, there's something here to satisfy every palate.

So, don your apron and embrace the culinary adventure that awaits in "Croctober: Asian Style - Volume One." These recipes are crafted to simplify your kitchen endeavors while elevating your dining experience with the vibrant, mouthwatering tastes of Asia. Enjoy the journey!

- Encourage readers to try out different recipes and enjoy a month of delicious Asian-style dishes in October.

As we wrap up our culinary exploration through the pages of "Croctober: Asian Style - Volume One," we wholeheartedly encourage you, dear reader, to embark on your own culinary adventure. Take this collection of Asian-style crockpot recipes and make October a month to savor.

Dive into the world of Asian cuisine with enthusiasm and curiosity, knowing that each recipe holds the potential to surprise and delight. Don't hesitate to experiment, adapt, and make these dishes your own. Swap ingredients to suit your preferences, and remember that the joy of cooking is in the journey as much as the destination.

As the weather turns cooler and the leaves begin to change, let the comforting aromas of these dishes fill your kitchen. Whether you're gathering with loved ones or savoring a meal for one, these recipes areadesigned to bring warmth and flavor to your table.

Throughout the month of Croctober, why not try a new recipe every few days? Challenge yourself to explore different Asian flavors and ingredients. Share your creations with friends and family, and relish the satisfaction of a delicious meal that you've prepared with love.

We hope these recipes become a source of inspiration and a catalyst for wonderful moments around the table. May "Croctober: Asian Style - Volume One" be the beginning of a culinary journey that brings joy, connection, and a deeper appreciation of the rich tapestry of Asian cuisine.

So, roll up your sleeves, gather your ingredients, and let the crockpot do the work as you embark on a month of delightful dining experiences. Here's to a Croctober filled with delicious Asian-style dishes and memorable moments! Enjoy every bite and savor the flavors of Asia at your own pace.

Recipe Card

NAME OF RECIPE

INGREDIENTS

SERVE

2 4 6 8

DIFFICULTY

INSTRUCTIONS

Vegetarian ☐
Dairy Free ☐
Low Carb ☐
Sugar Free ☐
Low Salt ☐

TIME TO PREPARE

REVIEW

Recipe Card

NAME OF RECIPE

SERVE

2　4　6　8

DIFFICULTY

Vegetarian ☐
Dairy Free ☐
Low Carb ☐
Sugar Free ☐
Low Salt ☐

TIME TO PREPARE

REVIEW

INGREDIENTS

INSTRUCTIONS

Recipe Card

NAME OF RECIPE	INGREDIENTS

SERVE

2 4 6 8

DIFFICULTY

Vegetarian ☐
Dairy Free ☐
Low Carb ☐
Sugar Free ☐
Low Salt ☐

TIME TO PREPARE

REVIEW

INSTRUCTIONS

Recipe Card

| NAME OF RECIPE | INGREDIENTS |

....

SERVE

| 2 | 4 | 6 | 8 |

....

DIFFICULTY

....

Vegetarian ☐
Dairy Free ☐
Low Carb ☐
Sugar Free ☐
Low Salt ☐

TIME TO PREPARE

....

REVIEW

INSTRUCTIONS

Recipe Card

NAME OF RECIPE	INGREDIENTS

SERVE

| 2 | 4 | 6 | 8 |

DIFFICULTY

INSTRUCTIONS

Vegetarian ☐
Dairy Free ☐
Low Carb ☐
Sugar Free ☐
Low Salt ☐

TIME TO PREPARE

REVIEW

Recipe Card

NAME OF RECIPE

SERVE

2 4 6 8

DIFFICULTY

Vegetarian ☐
Dairy Free ☐
Low Carb ☐
Sugar Free ☐
Low Salt ☐

TIME TO PREPARE

REVIEW

INGREDIENTS

INSTRUCTIONS

Recipe Card

NAME OF RECIPE	INGREDIENTS

SERVE

2   4   6   8

DIFFICULTY

Vegetarian ☐
Dairy Free ☐
Low Carb ☐
Sugar Free ☐
Low Salt ☐

INSTRUCTIONS

TIME TO PREPARE

REVIEW

Recipe Card

NAME OF RECIPE	INGREDIENTS

SERVE

2 4 6 8

DIFFICULTY

Vegetarian ☐
Dairy Free ☐
Low Carb ☐
Sugar Free ☐
Low Salt ☐

TIME TO PREPARE

REVIEW

INSTRUCTIONS

Recipe Card

<table>
<tr><td>

NAME OF RECIPE

....

SERVE

| 2 | 4 | 6 | 8 |

....

DIFFICULTY

....

Vegetarian ☐
Dairy Free ☐
Low Carb ☐
Sugar Free ☐
Low Salt ☐

TIME TO PREPARE

....

REVIEW

</td><td>

INGREDIENTS

INSTRUCTIONS

....
....
....
....
....
....
....
....

</td></tr>
</table>

Recipe Card

NAME OF RECIPE

SERVE

2   4   6   8

DIFFICULTY

Vegetarian ☐
Dairy Free ☐
Low Carb ☐
Sugar Free ☐
Low Salt ☐

TIME TO PREPARE

REVIEW

INGREDIENTS

INSTRUCTIONS

Recipe Card

NAME OF RECIPE	INGREDIENTS

SERVE

2 4 6 8

DIFFICULTY

- Vegetarian ☐
- Dairy Free ☐
- Low Carb ☐
- Sugar Free ☐
- Low Salt ☐

TIME TO PREPARE

REVIEW

INSTRUCTIONS

Recipe Card

NAME OF RECIPE

SERVE

| 2 | 4 | 6 | 8 |

DIFFICULTY

Vegetarian ☐
Dairy Free ☐
Low Carb ☐
Sugar Free ☐
Low Salt ☐

TIME TO PREPARE

REVIEW

INGREDIENTS

INSTRUCTIONS

Recipe Card

| NAME OF RECIPE | INGREDIENTS |

....

SERVE

2　4　6　8

....

DIFFICULTY

....

Vegetarian ☐
Dairy Free ☐
Low Carb ☐
Sugar Free ☐
Low Salt ☐

TIME TO PREPARE

....

REVIEW

INSTRUCTIONS

Recipe Card

NAME OF RECIPE

INGREDIENTS

SERVE

2 4 6 8

DIFFICULTY

Vegetarian ☐
Dairy Free ☐
Low Carb ☐
Sugar Free ☐
Low Salt ☐

INSTRUCTIONS

TIME TO PREPARE

REVIEW

Recipe Card

<table>
<tr><td>

NAME OF RECIPE

....

SERVE

2　4　6　8

....

DIFFICULTY

....

Vegetarian　☐
Dairy Free　☐
Low Carb　☐
Sugar Free　☐
Low Salt　☐

TIME TO PREPARE

....

REVIEW

</td><td>

INGREDIENTS

INSTRUCTIONS

....
....
....
....
....
....
....
....
....

</td></tr>
</table>

Recipe Card

NAME OF RECIPE	INGREDIENTS

SERVE

2   4   6   8

DIFFICULTY

Vegetarian ☐
Dairy Free ☐
Low Carb ☐
Sugar Free ☐
Low Salt ☐

TIME TO PREPARE

REVIEW

INSTRUCTIONS

Recipe Card

| NAME OF RECIPE | INGREDIENTS |

SERVE

2 4 6 8

DIFFICULTY

Vegetarian ☐
Dairy Free ☐
Low Carb ☐
Sugar Free ☐
Low Salt ☐

TIME TO PREPARE

REVIEW

INSTRUCTIONS

Recipe Card

| NAME OF RECIPE | INGREDIENTS |

SERVE

2 4 6 8

DIFFICULTY

Vegetarian ☐
Dairy Free ☐
Low Carb ☐
Sugar Free ☐
Low Salt ☐

TIME TO PREPARE

REVIEW

INSTRUCTIONS

Recipe Card

<table>
<tr><td>

NAME OF RECIPE

....

SERVE

| 2 | 4 | 6 | 8 |

....

DIFFICULTY

....

Vegetarian ☐
Dairy Free ☐
Low Carb ☐
Sugar Free ☐
Low Salt ☐

TIME TO PREPARE

....

REVIEW

</td><td>

INGREDIENTS

INSTRUCTIONS

....
....
....
....
....
....
....
....
....
....

</td></tr>
</table>

Recipe Card

NAME OF RECIPE	INGREDIENTS

SERVE

2 4 6 8

DIFFICULTY

Vegetarian ☐
Dairy Free ☐
Low Carb ☐
Sugar Free ☐
Low Salt ☐

INSTRUCTIONS

TIME TO PREPARE

REVIEW

NOTES

DATE

NOTES

DATE

NOTES

NOTES

NOTES

NOTES

 DATE

NOTES

NOTES

DATE

NOTES

DATE

NOTES

DATE

NOTES

NOTES

NOTES

NOTES

DATE

NOTES

DATE